Ventriloquist

Written by Professional Ventriloquist and Entertainer Dennis Patten

Illustrated by David Mostyn

© 1994 Henderson Publishing Limited

Henderson Publishing
Woodbridge, England

Welcome to the world of ventriloquism! A world in which you will have fun making your puppet talk and entertaining your family and friends. The time and effort spent in learning this new skill will be much rewarded when you hear the laughter and amusement created by the jokes and antics of your cardboard cut-out character.

I first became aware of dolls that talked when I was about five years old. My favourite uncle had given me a toy model of an American dummy called Charlie McCarthy. I still have it. It has a sawdust-filled body and a solid fixed head with a jaw made to move by pulling a shoe lace which comes out of a hole in the back of Charlie's neck. I couldn't do ventriloquism, of course, so I covered my moving lips by holding the dummy's head in front of my mouth every time Charlie spoke.

I next came across ventriloquism as an eleven year old, visiting my grandparents at the seaside. During the summer months a small troupe of entertainers would perform their shows in a little theatre on the promenade. One of the acts was a Ventriloquist who, prior to his performance, would sit his dummy on a chair at the side of the stage. I can still see it in my mind's eye, sitting there dressed as a page boy. I've been fascinated by these wooden-headed puppets ever since. A little while back I started to collect them, and I now have quite a number. You may have seen them on television as they are often in T.V. shows and films.

As a youngster I couldn't afford to buy a dummy so I made one from a newspaper and wire. It was a disaster! It was supposed to be a cheeky boy figure, but it looked like a monster from outer space! It's a shame that this book wasn't around when I was starting, it would have saved me a lot of time and trouble! Now making a vent figure just could not be easier - you just push out the puppet pieces provided and glue them together. This means that you can get started right away on learning to make it talk.

Who knows? Following the simple rules set out in this book could lead to greater things. You may like ventriloquism so much, and do it so well, that one day you will decide to use it as a means of earning your living. Even if you just want to learn it for fun, it makes an unusual hobby and 'Vents' are always in demand for charity shows.

There is actually a shortage of young Ventriloquists at the moment. A little while ago, a television company wanted young performers and we could only find one in the whole of the country!

Practise each lesson regularly and master each step before moving on to the next. When you are able to converse with your puppet, learn a string of jokes and riddles and polish up your routine before you try it out in front of your family.

Before we start on the first lesson, it might be a good idea to tell you something about the ancient art of ventriloquism.

There is more than one type of ventriloquism, and to tell all there is to know would need a very large book, many times the size of this one. The lessons explained here are for learning the type known as 'near ventriloquism'. This is for giving a voice to a dummy held about 30cms away from the performer, ideal for the puppets supplied in the middle section of this book.

Ancient art?

Yes, it is very ancient. It has a mention in the Bible, and was around as far back as 3000 B.C. Just like its sister art of magic and conjuring, it was first used to deceive and mislead ignorant people. Religions and tribal leaders used it to impress and control their followers. The Chiefs would appear to carry on conversations with stone and wooden idols or Gods. Anyone who could shout to a cloud in the heavens, or speak to a sacred tree and get an answer back, must be someone to be obeyed!

If the truth were known, the 'Great Ones' didn't even have to be too good at lip control either! Their lips could have been covered by hands cupped around their mouth to shout a greeting. All they needed to do was change the sound of their voice for the reply.

Later on, ventriloquism became an entertainment, and was practised by travelling entertainers performing at fairs and in inns. A popular item was the talking hand. This has been depicted in many old prints of the period.

Radio came along and stars were soon made of Edgar Bergen, with his dummy Charlie McCarthy, in America, and Peter Brough and his figure, in England. Edgar Bergen moved into films and became even more famous in the cinema. Toy copies were made of his dummy 'Charlie' - it was one of these that my uncle gave me. These days, with television and the close-up lens, the Ventriloquist needs to have better lip control than ever before.

In the 1800's, Ventriloquists started to appear in the music halls. It was a common sight to see five or six dummies on stage at the same time with the performer moving up and down behind them, pulling the strings and having them converse with each other. The traditional two person act of the performer and his talkative partner didn't come into being until about 1900.

Those simple deceived followers that I mentioned earlier were not the only people to be misled. The folk who put a name to ventriloquism also got it wrong! The word ventriloquism comes from two Latin words; 'venter' meaning 'belly', and 'loquer' meaning 'to speak'. Translated literally ventriloquism means 'belly speak', or 'to speak from the belly'. You don't need to be a Doctor to know that this is impossible - still, it is an illusion.

An illusion?

Yes, it is just that, which is why you will find that many Ventriloquists are also performing Magicians, or at least have an interest in magic. Ventriloquists' dummies, for instance, are mostly found in magic shops.

Ventriloquism is an illusion in which sounds are made to appear to come from any source other than from the performer. To create this illusion, the 'Near Ventriloquist' makes use of the fact that the eye is attracted by a moving object, which is why a simple wave (a moving hand) enables us to gain the attention of someone across a crowded room. In the Ventriloquist's case, it is the dummy, or puppet, which moves. This takes the audience's eye away from the performer's mouth so that any slight movement is not noticed.

At the same time, the puppet's jaw is made to open and close in unison with the speech to give the impression that the figure is actually talking. It goes without saying that the better the lip control of the Ventriloquist, the better the illusion.

Now that you have some background knowledge of the art of ventriloquism, it's time to get down to learning to do it yourself.

Turn to the middle pages of this book and carefully push out the puppet pieces. Glue the basic shape together, following the instructions carefully, and fit the various parts until you find a character that appeals to you. I like the monkey puppet, so I've glued the eyes, ears, nose and teeth permanently in place. I've decided to call my puppet 'Hunkey Dorey' or 'Hunkey the Monkey'.

Put your puppet away somewhere safe for a while as it's not needed for the first two lessons. Ready? Right, off we go then with …

Such a tongue twister is the word 'ventriloquism' that, over the years, it has been shortened to 'vent'. In fact, in the trade, the word 'vent' can mean ventriloquist, ventriloquism or ventriloquial. A boy or girl puppet with a moving jaw is referred to as either a vent dummy, a vent figure or a vent doll. An animal which can talk is called a 'vent puppet'. Other expressions used are: gag, which means a joke or something which is funny; sight bit, means visual joke and routine describes whatever the vent and puppet say and do.

Lesson 1 - Keeping those lips still!

First of all, tell your parents what you are doing and they will help you to find somewhere quiet, away from other people, so that you can study. As you will also need a large looking glass, a bedroom and a dressing table fitted with a mirror is usually the answer.

Sit down in front of the mirror, about 2ft (60cms) away, and try holding your mouth in basic position 'A'.

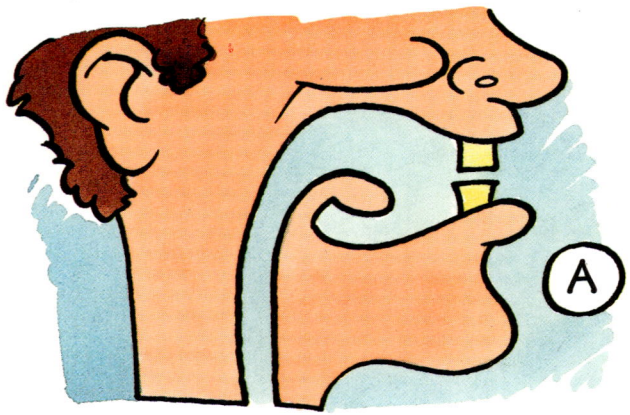

Relax your lips, holding them slightly apart, and touch the lower edge of your upper middle teeth gently on your lower lip, allowing your tongue to move freely behind your teeth. Now, without moving your jaw or your lips, but using your tongue normally, say, in your usual voice:

"How do I sound?"

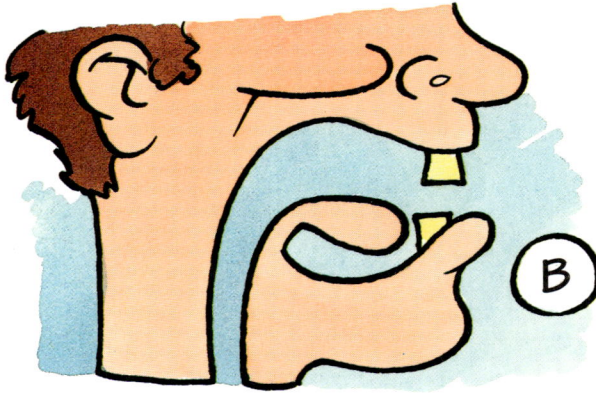

The answer will be, O.K. but not that clear. Time to try basic position 'B'. Hold your mouth as before but, this time, move your upper teeth a fraction away from your lower lip. Once again, say:

"How do I sound?"

The result, this time, will be much clearer but needing more power. To obtain that, hold position 'B', as before, but draw in a deep breath. Say the words once more, breathing out at the same time:

"How do I sound?"

You will find your voice is clear and much stronger.

The story so far ......

Correct breathing, along with basic positions 'A' and 'B', is the formula for speaking without moving your lips. You use basic position 'B' for the easy words and position 'A' for the difficult ones.

Normally, when we speak, our upper lip touches our lower lip to pronounce words. In position 'A', it is our upper teeth which touch our lower lip to speak.

Take the word 'wait' for example. In natural speech the lips move forward and touch for 'w' and open for 'ait' (Fig. 1). To say it without moving your lips you hold position 'A' and say 'wait', pushing your tongue forward and breathing out at the same time (Fig. 2).

Lesson 2 - Easy is easy but peasy isn't.

Take up position 'B' and look into the mirror. Using your own voice, and keeping your lips still, recite the letters of the alphabet. If you say it through a number of times, you will be able to do it quite well, except for 'b', 'm', 'p', 'v' and 'w'. To say these sounds, Ventriloquists have replaced them with other words which can be made to sound almost the same as the original ones.

Let's take them in turn:

'b' is pronounced 'vhee'.

This is done by lowering the upper teeth to position 'A' to momentarily touch the lower lip as you breathe out, saying 'vhee'. To start with you must practise and practise to try and make it sound as much like 'b' as you can. This is the same for the other sounds:

'm' is pronounced 'eng'
'p' is pronounced 'fhee' (breathe it)
'v' is pronounced 'vhee' (breathe it)
'w' is pronounced 'duvvle-you'

In saying these sounds the top lip remains still whilst the upper teeth touch the lower lip in its place.

Let us try to say an actual word. The word 'pickle'. To say 'pickle', you touch your upper teeth to your lower lip and say 'ffickle', trying to make it sound as near to the word as possible. Now it could be that your pronunciation of 'ffickle' may not be all that convincing, but put into the middle of a sentence like "I've just had a cheese and ffickle sandwich," and it will be more acceptable. The familiar words which lead up to the difficult sound allows your friends to accept 'ffickle' for the expected 'pickle'.

It's a known fact that people hear what they expect to hear. Ask your dad to 'ffass' the salt at the dinner table and I will guarantee he'll pass it without hesitation.

This Lesson No. 2 is quite the most important, that is why you must practise saying 'b', 'p', 'm', 'v' and 'w' over and over again, first by themselves then in complete 'a-z', until you are happy with the result. When you are satisfied pick up your paper puppet and start on Lesson 3.

Lesson 3 - Getting to know your puppet

Take up your position again in front of the mirror and insert your hand into the head of the puppet. The head is made to take your fingers in the top half and your thumb in the lower jaw. Hold the head up next to you, with your elbow held downwards. Keeping the top of the head still, drop your thumb: this will allow the bottom jaw to fall open. Close your thumb and the jaw will shut. You have to open and close the puppet's mouth once for each letter. The letter 'w' needs to have the jaw open and closed three times, one for each syllable.

Look in the mirror and run through the alphabet again, this time treating it as a routine. You start with 'a', speaking naturally and moving your lips, and your partner replies 'b', with your lips still. You say 'c' (moving lips) and the puppet 'd' (lips still). Keep going until you reach 'z', then start the whole thing again, but varying it by letting your pal say 'a' first and you replying 'b' and so on.

It's time to move on, and the next step is to have your puppet speak simple phrases. Here is a routine for you to practise in which your puppet's lines consist of nothing more than letters of the alphabet. As you know, I quite like the Monkey puppet, so I've used his name in the script. You can easily adapt this to suit the particular animal you have chosen to use.

In this routine you say the lines marked V for Ventriloquist and your puppet, those marked P for puppet.

V   Hi there, Mr. Monkey.
P   i i (Aye, Aye)
V   How are you?
P   o.k. n.u. (O.K. and you?)
V   Fine. I'm really fit.
P   i.c.u.r. (I see you are)
V   I've been on a programme.
P   t.v? (T.V.?)
V   No, P.T..
P   p.t? (P.T.?)
V   Yes, P.T.. Physical Training.
P   o. (Oh.)
V   Anyway, never mind that. I've called you here to find a name for you.
P   y? (Why?)
V   I can't keep calling you Mr. Monkey.
P   o.i.c. (Oh, I see)
V   Would you like a name?
P   s. (Yes)
V   How about Marmaduke?
P   e.e.e. (laughs)
V   Don't laugh. The name suits you.
P   o.k. (O.K.)
V   Hold on, here's a good name - Hunkey Dorey.
P   o.g. (Oh gee)
V   I name this animal Hunkey the Monkey.

CURTAIN

Practise this script each day in front of a mirror until you can do it well. Little and often is the secret, but for no longer than 15 minutes each session. Don't tire yourself otherwise it will cease to be enjoyable.

Lesson 4 - Finding a voice

Up until now you have been talking in one voice - your own. Now you must find another different voice for your puppet so as to complete the illusion of two people talking. The character you choose will decide which type of sound you create. The elephant, for example, would have a deep voice, while the monkey a high one. Remember, any voice you use should be produced without strain on your throat or expression on your face.

Start by holding your mouth in the basic position 'B' and say something in your normal voice. Keep saying the phrase, moving the sound into the back of your throat and up in the area behind your nose. This will give a higher pitch to the voice. To get a deep voice, still move the sound to the back of the throat, but this time set it as low as possible.

If you get no success with the above system, try to imitate an unusual voice of someone you know, or a cartoon character. You may not actually sound like that person, but you will end up with a voice which contrasts with your own.

Choosing a name

After deciding on a voice for your puppet, you must think up a name; a name that has not been used before by anyone else. Also, as you will be repeating it many times in your routines, one that is easy for your puppet to say.

When you have both a voice and a name for your puppet, run through the previous exercises again and again. Practise until you can change voices quickly so that it sounds as though two people are talking.

Lesson 5 - Moving your puppet

To add to the illusion that your puppet is alive, you must keep it moving all the time it is on view, even when it's not talking. It must never be seen still, so it's a good idea to have some cover, say a box with a lift-up lid, so your friends cannot actually see you putting the puppet on to your hand.

When you are talking, make your puppet look towards you, and when he replies, look towards him. You can make him appear bashful by tilting the head forward slightly, or go to sleep by tilting it well down so the eyes cannot be seen. A snore or two will help the effect. Shake the puppet while the head is bent forwards to give the impression of sobbing. Open his jaws wide and he will yawn. Look in the mirror and see what movements and moods you can create.

You must look upon your character as a real person: if you do, so will your audience.

Lesson 6 - Creating a routine

This is not as difficult as it sounds as long as you can find the right jokes. Jokes are everywhere: comics, books, T.V. and school pals are all good sources for funny lines.

Start a collection right away and write them down under various headings, like 'Cars', 'Work', 'School', 'Animals' and so on. Then, if you want a script about School, for instance, you just have to look at the appropriate sheet.

Before you can use the jokes, they'll have to be rewritten for two people to say, with the puppet getting most, if not all, of the punch lines. To show how it's done, let's take the following half dozen jokes:

Do you know they gave me the sack first day at work? I'm a Postman.

Did you hear the story of the cornflakes? It's a cereal (serial).

I'm on house-to-house deliveries now. I don't like it much but it's better than tramping the streets.

A. Where do you find the Andes?
B. At the end of my armies (arms).

Do you remember that watch you gave me? Rustproof, dustproof and waterproof? Well, it caught fire!

If you have referees in football and umpires in cricket, what do you have in bowls? Goldfish.

When they are rewritten for two people, the Ventriloquist (V) and the Puppet (P), they read like this:

V How's your new job?
P *I got the sack first day.*
V Got the sack first day? What sort of job is that?
P *Postman.*
V Funny chap. Tell me, are you on house-to-house deliveries?
P *Yes.*
V Do you like it?
P *It's better than tramping the streets!*
V I asked for that.
P *Do you know the time?*
V You should know the time, I gave you a watch for Christmas.
P *I know.*
V It was a good watch too. Rustproof, dustproof and water proof.
P *I know.*

V What happened to it?
P It caught fire.
V Sorry. Anyway, why do you want to know the time?
P There's a good show on telly.
V What's it called?
P The Crazy Cornflake. It's on every week.

V Every week?
P Yes, it's a cereal.
V Boom, boom! I prefer quiz shows because I know all the answers.
P You would!
V Here's a question. Where do you find the Andes?
P At the end of my armies.

V No, no, no!
P Here's one for you.
V I'm listening.
P If you have referees in football,
V Yes.
P And umpires in cricket,

V Yes.
P What do you have in bowls?
V I give up.
P Goldfish.
V Oh dear! (groan) Say 'goodbye' Hunkey.
P Goodbye Hunkey.
CURTAIN

You can see that linking dialogue has joined together single jokes to form a two person conversation.

So ends the six lessons in 'Near Ventriloquism'. If you have faithfully practised all the exercises set out, you should by now be able to give a short, but entertaining performance for your family and friends.

As mentioned previously, a Ventriloquist should always regard his or her dummy as a real person. With this in mind, I asked each of the puppets supplied with this book to give their favourite jokes and riddles to help you start your gag collection.

Dog

V What kind of dog goes round and round in circles before lying down?
P A watchdog. He winds himself up.

P It's raining cats and dogs now.
V How do you know?
P I just stepped into a poodle.

P Doctor, I keep thinking I'm a dog.
V How long has this been going on?
P Since I was a puppy.

V I call my dog Isaiah.
P Why is that?
V One eye's higher than the other.

P Now you see me, now you don't. What am I?
V A black poodle on a zebra crossing.

V What has four legs and flies?
P Two pairs of trousers.

V My name's Rover. What's yours?
P I'm not sure. I think it's Down Boy.

V I had to take my dog to the vet.
P Was he mad?
V Well, he wasn't too pleased, I can tell you!

Mr. Bowler

V You have exactly the same answer as the girl next to you.
P I know. We used the same pen!

P Do you know, I went to night school so I could learn to read in the dark.

P Dear Mum, I'm writing this slowly because I know you cannot read very fast.

V What has four wheels and flies?
P A dustcart.

V How would you like your hair cut, sir?
P Off.

V Did you hear about the motorist who thought he was a magician?
P He drove up the road and turned into a side street.

P I've borrowed my neighbour's trumpet.
V But you can't play the trumpet!
P I know, but neither can he while I've got it.

V What goes from branch to branch and wears a bowler hat?
P A Bank Manager.

Monkey

P I spent all day yesterday making faces at the goldfish. I know that's silly, but he started it.

P Every loaf is untouched by human hand. The Baker is a monkey.

P Do you have frog's legs?
V Yes sir.
P Then hop into the kitchen and get me a sandwich.

P What's the cure for water on the brain?
V A tap on the head.

V Now then, you little Monkey, how did that teapot get broken?
P I was cleaning my catapult and it went off by accident.

P My teacher told me off because I couldn't remember where the Eiffel Tower was.
V Serves you right. Remember where you put things next time.

P This lobster has only one claw.
V I know sir, it's been in a fight.
P Well, take it away and fetch me the winner!

V Where do monkeys buy their hats?
P At a Jungle Sale.

Pig

V What do you use to treat a pig with a sore trotter?
P Oinkment.

P My wife's got a good head for money.
V Really?
P Yes, it has a slot in the top.

V What do you call an excellent farmer?
P Outstanding in his field.

P Do you believe in free speech?
V I certainly do.
P Super! May I use your 'phone?

P Knock, knock.
V Who's there?
P Cook.
V Cook who?
P That's the first one I've heard this year.

P I can't see very far.
V What's that up there in the sky?
P The moon.
V How far do you want to see?

V Why was the farmer cross?
P Someone trod on his corn!

V What do you get when a pig rings you up?
P Crackling on the line.

V What do pigs have that no other animals have?
P Piglets.

Elephant

V Can an elephant jump higher than a lamp post?
P I say, lamp posts can't jump.

P Nurse, nurse, I keep seeing pink elephants!
V Have you seen the doctor?
P No, only the pink elephants.

V How do you catch an elephant?
P Hide behind a bush and make a noise like a peanut.

P What do you get if you cross an elephant with a goldfish?
V Swimming trunks.

P I know a baby who gained 10lbs in two weeks by drinking elephant's milk.
V Whose baby was it?
P The elephant's.

P Peanuts must be fattening. I've never seen a skinny elephant.

V Why are elephants so wrinkled?
P They're too heavy for the ironing board.

V I know what I'd give a seasick elephant.
P What?
V Lots of room!

Wizard

P Did you hear about the Magician with five legs?
V His trousers fitted him like a glove!

P I may be a clever Wizard, but my budgie can do something I can't do.
Have a bath in a saucer.

V What's your son going to be when he passes all his Magic Circle exams?
P A pensioner.

V What do you call a space Magician?
P A flying Sorcerer.

V Are these beans quick growing?
P I'll say. As soon as you've planted them, jump well clear!

V This is a one way street. Didn't you see the arrows?
P I didn't even see the Indians.

V Who was the biggest robber in history?
P Atlas – he held up the world.

V What do the police force use at lunch?
P Truncheon vouchers.

P The other day, as I sat lonely and friendless, I heard a voice say to me "Cheer up, things could be worse.". So I cheered up and, sure enough, things got worse!

Making the most of your puppet

You can add a great deal to the appearance of your chosen character by providing it with a body or a neck and box. Here's how:

The Handkerchief Body

Not only does this enhance your dummy, it also prevents the audience from seeing your hand entering the Puppet's head.

> **You'll need:**
> a gentleman's (15 inch) square handkerchief
> card bow tie and hands
> a pipe cleaner or a strip of card
> single and double-sided sticky tape

The hanky should, if possible, match the colour of the chosen puppet.
Fasten the hanky by the middle portion of the top hem into the upper jaw of the puppet. Use regular sticky tape. (see Fig. 1)

Fold over the upper corners of the handkerchief and, using double sided tape, fix the hands and bow tie in position (Fig. 2).

Finish off by folding back the lower hem with the pipe cleaner or card strip inside it and stick it back with regular sticky tape (Fig. 3).

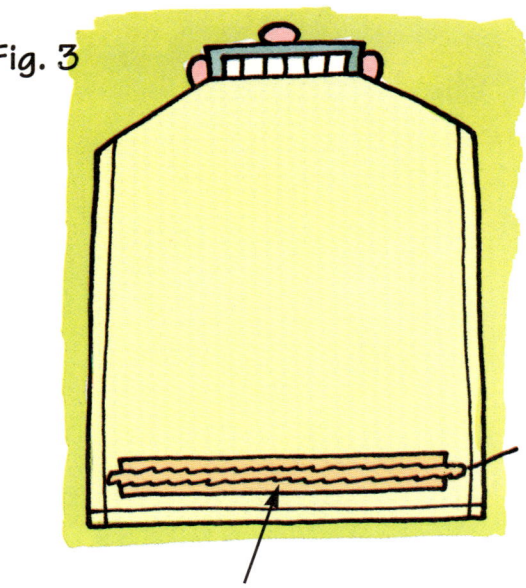

PIPE CLEANER OR CARD STRIP

Fashion the lower hem in a half round shape for completion (Fig. 4).

BEND LOWER HEM INTO A CURVE SHAPE

The neck and box

This is an ideal set-up for a puppet because much fun can be had with the character hiding in the box or peeping out under the lid when the Vent isn't looking.

You'll need:
a squarish cardboard box (you could join together a couple of cereal boxes)
an old sock or ankle warmers
a card bow tie
double-sided sticky tape

Take the box and carefully cut out a hole in the back using a pair of scissors (Fig. 5).

Fig. 5

Slide the ankle warmer onto your arm, or use the old sock with a hole cut out for your thumb, attach the bow tie with double sided tape (Figs. 6 & 7).

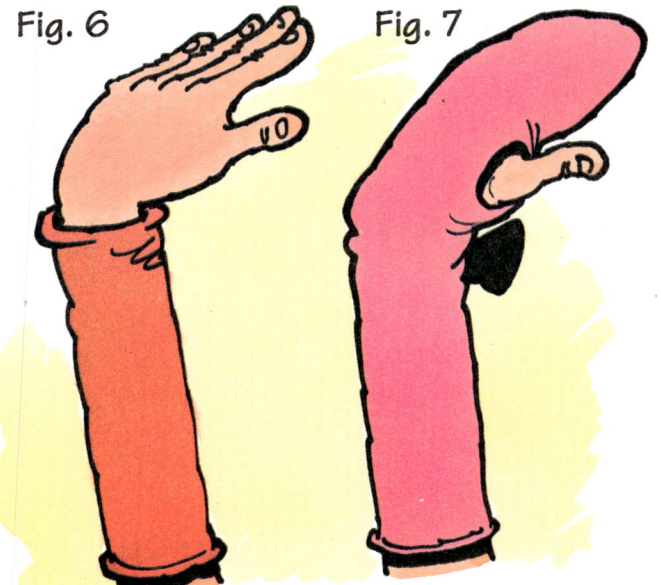
Fig. 6   Fig. 7

Then insert your arm through the hole in the back of the box and fit the puppet head in place on your hand (Fig. 8).

Have fun!

Fig. 8